Learning to Follow:

Encountering Jesus
in the Gospels

"The one who looks at Me

is seeing the One Who sent Me."

John 12:45

This Bible study is dedicated to Jesus Christ,
the One Who loves us and invites us follow Him.

Karen Wycoff Watson 2019

When Jesus spoke again to the people, He said,
"I am the Light of the world.
Whoever follows Me will never walk in darkness,
but will have the light of life."
John 8:12 NIV

My sheep listen to My Voice; I know them, and they follow Me.
I give them eternal life, and they shall never perish;
no one will snatch them out of My hand.
John 10:27-28 NIV

TABLE OF CONTENTS

INTRODUCTION

This Bible study consists of encounters between people and Jesus from the pages of the Gospels in the New Testament. The Gospels, the Books of Matthew, Mark, Luke and John, are the accounts of Jesus' life on earth. Each of these men told the story of Jesus' life from their own unique perspective. All four gospel writers provide rich insight as they recorded what happened during this most pivotal time in human history, when Jesus Christ, the Son of God, lived, as a man, on earth. John and Matthew were invited to follow Jesus and as they said yes, found themselves among the 12, Jesus' earliest disciples. Matthew had been a tax collector (see Matthew 9:9) and John, a fishermen (see Mark 1:19-20). Mark and Luke came along a bit later. Mark was a devoted companion of Peter's (see 1 Peter 5:13) and Luke was a trusted and faithful friend to Paul (see 2 Timothy 4:11). These four were privileged to tell the story of the most influential, purposeful, astonishingly brilliant life ever lived.

As you read the passages of scripture provided, you are encouraged to try to imagine yourself with Jesus, back then. As we read these accounts imaginatively we can discern what it might have been like to hear, see, even touch Jesus. We can think about how His life might have impacted our own. As we read in this way, we can be touched by Jesus, in our own, here and now lives. Jesus said in John 12:45 (NIV), *"The one who looks at Me is seeing the One Who sent Me."* As we study the life of Jesus, the lived out love and grace of the Father are clearly revealed.

This study is designed to help you look closely at the events of Jesus' life. You will notice the people He interacted with: His disciples, the huge crowds of people, the self-righteous religious elite, as well as the many individuals who came to Him for a myriad of reasons. There were those who loved and followed Him, those who were confused by Him, those who were resistant to Him and everything in-between. Reading the Gospels with attention to detail, quickly reveals that people in Jesus' day weren't much different from us. Their struggles and questions, pain and pride, joys and heartaches, their unbelief and distorted images of God were the same things we grapple with now. The stuff of humanity. If we honestly look within ourselves we can learn from these people, from what they got right and what they got wrong.

You can also learn from Jesus' way of life. You will see He lived with unwavering purpose in order to bring hope and healing to the world. He lived in complete obedience to His Father in heaven, as He made salvation available for all mankind. He was intentional in every word and deed. He didn't let anyone or anything deter Him from His mission to bring the Kingdom of God to earth.

INTRODUCTION

Jesus' character is clearly displayed as He brought (and continues to bring) His Kingdom life, salvation, to our lost and broken world. His tenderness, patience, grace, kindness, faithfulness, brilliant wisdom, justice, compassion and His love are apparent. You will notice timing in what He did. He was never in a hurry with people. He was fully present with them, regardless of their lifestyle, their ignorance, or their neediness. No interruption seemed to inconvenience Him. When conversing with someone, He could get to the heart of the matter with one or two simple questions regardless of the actual question they may have asked Him. He knew exactly what they needed, even as they didn't know themselves.

He knows our deepest needs as well. Nothing is hidden from Him (and He loves us regardless). He knows us all, personally, inside and out. Jesus was (and is) eminently relational. It is interesting to note as we study scripture, the many ways God is described, which are clearly relational. Father, Bridegroom, Counselor, Master, High Priest, Friend, Teacher, Savior, Comforter, Shepherd, Guide, Strengthener, Redeemer, Immanuel (God with us). None of these words involve just one; they only work in relationship. We are the ones on the other side of these words of connection. Make no mistake, God desires for us to be in a close, day to day, relationship with Him. This Bible study is designed to help you draw closer to the Lord.

Jesus' rhythm of life, is worth observing. One important thing to note is how He got away to spend time with His Father in prayer and solitude. He knew when He needed to be replenished with what only His Father in heaven could give Him. We too can respond to God's gracious invitation to come to Him, which is found in both the Old and New Testament.

One of God's Invitations in the Old Testament ~ Isaiah 55:1-3 (NLT)

"Is anyone thirsty?
Come and drink— even if you have no money!
Come, take your choice of wine or milk— it's all free!
Why spend your money on food that does not give you strength?
Why pay for food that does you no good?
Listen to Me, and you will eat what is good. You will enjoy the finest food.
"Come to Me with your ears wide open.Listen, and you will find life.
I will make an everlasting covenant with you.
I will give you all the unfailing love I promised to David."

INTRODUCTION

One of God's Invitations in New Testament ~ Matthew 11:28-30 (MSG)

"Are you tired? Worn out? Burned out on religion?
Come to Me. Get away with Me and you'll recover your life.
I'll show you how to take a real rest. Walk with Me and work with Me—watch how I do it.
Learn the unforced rhythms of grace. I won't lay anything heavy or ill-fitting on you.
Keep company with Me and you'll learn to live freely and lightly."

This is not an invitation to remember only when we are exhausted or stressed out. It is an ongoing invitation we need to accept with regularity. It is in coming to the Lord we receive what our hearts truly yearn for. We build a solid foundation of relationship, of intimacy, with Him by spending time with Him. It is just like any relationship in this way. It is in our time with Jesus He is able to restore us, reveal truth to us, and give us the soul comfort and rest our hearts crave. As we are with Him, He influences us and shapes our hearts to reflect His. He resets our priorities, and fills us with what only He can give. Unconditional love. And make no mistake. There is no better fuel than the love of God to get us through the ups and downs of life.

Being in these Gospel passages is a great way to spend time with the Lord. As you go through this study, you are encouraged to read, ponder, meditate on, believe and pray scripture with the understanding the Bible works deeply in our hearts and minds if we allow it to. This is not about gathering information about God, although this will happen. It is about allowing God to speak into your life and change you, from the inside, out. It is about transformation. Paul tells us in 1 Thessalonians 2:13 (NIV), *"And we also thank God continually because, when you received the Word of God, which you heard from us, you accepted it not as a human word, but as it actually is, the Word of God, which is indeed at work in you who believe."*

The Bible is active and alive (check out Hebrews 4:12). What the Lord says to each of us will be different as we are all in different ages, stages, and seasons of our lives. But no matter where we are, we can learn to trust God wants to lovingly intersect our lives with His Word, daily, as we navigate the ups and downs of life with His Word. If Jesus needed to regularly, be alone with God, then how much more do we? We need His Word to be fresh in our hearts and minds in order to live well. Amazingly, at some point, as we spend more and more time with God, we find ourselves doing life differently. We do it better. We find that our hearts are more content as we learn to trust Him, more and more.

INTRODUCTION

The truth is, we all live from the inside out. Our insides direct most of what we say and do as we interact with the world around us. It is our insides we attend to as we are with the Lord. Too often, Christians try to do life, on their own, without seeking the Lord. They practice "try harder religion" and spend little or no time in His Word and prayer (talking and listening to Him) and then wonder why they are burned out, resentful, and disillusioned. If we discipline ourselves to spend intentional time with the Lord, then we are richly blessed and we're able to bless others.

As we spend prayerful time in Scripture, being receptive to it, we begin to see the difference between our own frail and faulty wisdom and the wisdom of God. We grow in our understanding of Who God is, the nature of His character. It also changes the way we think of ourselves. Our identities are more and more grounded in the truth of who we are as beloved children of God. His love settles down deep within us, which gives us great strength to withstand the storms of life. We start to notice how we might make a difference in the world, offering tangible love to those around us. Our lives begin to bear good fruit as His love spills through and out of us, as overflow.

In Acts we see the powerful effect being with Jesus had on His early followers, particularly, John and Peter, as they were testifying on behalf of Jesus before the skeptical rulers and elders of their time. Those rulers and elders couldn't believe these men were unschooled fishermen as we see in Acts 4:13 (AMP) where it says, "*Now when they saw the boldness and unfettered eloquence of Peter and John and perceived that they were unlearned and untrained in the schools [common men with no educational advantages], they marveled; and they recognized that they had been with Jesus.*" These men weren't fitting the mold of uneducated fishermen. They were different in perceivable and amazing ways. They were eloquent in speech and they were bold. Those rulers and elders couldn't help but connect the dots and understand this was all a result of these men having been with Jesus.

This can be the same for us as well, as we spend time with the Lord. This is how we become the transforming people God uses to reach the world (those around us) with His impeccable love and grace. 2 Corinthians 3:16-18 (NIV) describes this process, "*But whenever anyone turns to the Lord, the veil is taken away. Now the Lord is the Spirit, and where the Spirit of the Lord is, there is freedom. And we all, who with unveiled faces contemplate the Lord's glory, are being transformed into His image with ever-increasing glory, which comes from the Lord, who is the Spirit.*"

INTRODUCTION

It is important to remember the transformation of our souls is a process. A long one at that. None of us is perfect. As followers of Jesus, we are in a life-long process of growing and maturing in the Lord. The amazing thing is God somehow seems to use us in-spite of our struggles and imperfections as we continue to seek Him in our day-to-day lives. He is perfectly content to let us help bring His Kingdom come, to the world around us, despite our shortcomings. He somehow makes it all good.

May you be richly blessed through this study, as you discover the riches of the abundant life Jesus came to bring us. May you delight in the depths of His forever love, finding it indeed brings us peace that passes all understanding (see Philippians 4:7). May you enjoy His Presence with you as you accept His gracious invitation to come to Him, to follow Him.

Karen Wycoff Watson
Carlsbad, California
2019

DETAILS

➤ God leads and guides us by His Spirit as we prayerfully seek Him in His Word. Before you start, ask the Holy Spirit to direct your heart and your mind as you read. In John 16:13a (NIV) Jesus promises us, *"But when He, the Spirit of truth, comes, He will guide you into all the truth."*

➤ This study can be done alone, as part of your personal devotions. You can go at the pace you want, spending as much time in each passage as you like.

➤ Doing the study in a group is wonderful as well. You can enjoy great conversation as everyone shares their personal insights. If you use this in a group you will want to decide how many passages of scripture per week to do. It is designed to be flexible so how fast you go is up to you. If you do it as a group, it is helpful to have ground rules. This helps the group develop as a safe place for everyone to open up and share. Such as:

   • Respect the opinions and insights of others even if they are different from your own, remembering we are all in process.

   • Avoid trying to fix or change others during group time. Do not give unsolicited advice, trusting the Holy Spirit to be at work in everyone. Focus on tending to your own heart.

   • Be a good listener in your group, respecting everyone's time to be heard. Be careful to not dominate the conversation; everyone's voice is important.

   • If you have limited meeting time, keep sharing and prayers brief enough to give everyone a chance to be heard. Never pressure anyone to pray or share.

   • Nothing you hear in the group is to be repeated outside the group. Betraying confidence even in the guise of concerned prayer or sharing is never appropriate.

   • Share your own story not anyone else's. Your small group time should be about what you are learning and what God is doing in your own life.

   • Work at avoiding divisive subjects. God calls us to live as His followers, in unity with one another.

   • *"Out of respect for Christ, be courteously reverent to one another."* Ephesians 5:21 (MSG)

DETAILS

➤ Work on imagining yourself in the passages. Envision yourself hearing and seeing the things Jesus is saying and doing. What do you notice? Think about what you might have been thinking and how you might have been feeling if you had been there then. The Bible frequently mentions those who listened to Jesus speak were amazed. What amazes you? What speaks to you?

➤ The scriptures provided are from various translations of the Bible. Feel free to look up the passages in other translations you enjoy, as reading from more than one translation can bring fresh, new awarenesses around what you are reading.

➤ Make note of questions you have, things you don't understand. Get comfortable lingering in questions. There are many that take time and patience to work through, not to mention the ones no one will ever know the answer to.

➤ Feel free to find other passages of scripture that relate to what you are learning. You might want to look up the meaning and uses of words that intrigue you as well.

➤ You can use this study like a journal. Underline and circle things that stand out to you. Use the space provided to write and process what you are learning. Be completely honest as you read and write. Jot down questions and insights. You might want to write some things out as prayers.

➤ This study is very much about quiet listening to the Lord. God uses His Word to meet you right where you are. Wisdom, guidance, encouragement, hope and much more await you in the pages of scripture. Blanks to fill in and commentary are great, but this study is more about helping you linger and listen, in order to hear what God might want to say to you, personally, as you read, study, listen, and pray through the passages. When you complete this book, you can use the simple questions you will be using with each passage, to study any book of the Bible.

➤ Bible study is never something to check off your to-do list. Think of it like you're going to spend time with a dear friend. Jesus is, after all, our dearest Friend. John heard Jesus say, *"No longer do I call you servants, for the servant does not know what his master is doing; but I have called you friends, for all that I have heard from my Father I have made known to you."* John 15:15 (ESV) Let's face it; this is an astonishing statement. Lingering with a friend like Jesus is something incredibly life giving.

DETAILS

➤ At the end of some of the passages there are other passages you can look up. They relate in some way to the passage you are in and will give you an expanded understanding around your reading.

➤ Don't stress about how much time you have. Just do the best you can to find a rhythm of being in the Word that fits the season of your life. Jesus knows (as a loving friend knows) how much time you have; you can trust Him to help you make the most of that time.

➤ Keep in mind that as you do this study, you aren't just seeking Biblical knowledge, although you'll get that. The ultimate goal of being with God in His Word is personal transformation. He wants us to become more and more like Him. The Message has a great way of paraphrasing Romans 12:1-2 (MSG), in order to help us remember what we learn from the Bible is to be lived out. *"So here's what I want you to do, God helping you: Take your everyday, ordinary life—your sleeping, eating, going-to-work, and walking-around life—and place it before God as an offering. Embracing what God does for you is the best thing you can do for Him. Don't become so well-adjusted to your culture that you fit into it without even thinking. Instead, fix your attention on God. You'll be changed from the inside out. Readily recognize what He wants from you, and quickly respond to it. Unlike the culture around you, always dragging you down to its level of immaturity, God brings the best out of you, develops well-formed maturity in you."* As you are in this study, you are encouraged to think about how what you are learning is to be worked out in your "walking- around life."

➤ On the next pages are ways to read and reflect as you do this study. Do your best to follow them, writing your insights as you go. Please notice you are asked to read and reread the passages of scripture. You will be tempted to skip the important reading and rereading part of the process. Don't give in to that temptation; you will be amazed at how much more you will discover with each reading.

WAYS TO READ AND REFLECT

➤ <u>ONE</u>   <u>PRAYERFULLY READ AND CONSIDER THIS QUESTION</u>

~WHAT ARE MY INITIAL OBSERVATIONS FROM THIS FIRST READING?

Read the passage slowly and prayerfully, with an open heart and mind. Ask the LORD to speak to you as you read. Think of interacting with the Him, as in a personal conversation as you read. Listen for what the Lord might be saying to you.

Jot down your initial observations. Don't over think this, just write bullet points.
A few things you could look for are:
• Questions you have • Insights you discover • Things that touches your heart
• Confusing things • Clarifying things • Themes • Significant details • Comforting or correcting truths • Something you are glad to be reminded of • Promises to hold on to

➤ <u>TWO</u>   <u>READ AND CONSIDER THIS QUESTION</u>

~ WHAT CAN I SEE IN PEOPLE I RECOGNIZE IN MYSELF?

Notice the people in the story. Jesus' disciples. The Pharisees. The crowds. Those who come to Him with questions or problems. What are their attitudes towards Him? What emotions do you see in them? What do you think they learned from Him? What did they miss? What kinds of changes do you see in them after their time with Jesus? How can you relate to them? What can you learn from their time with Jesus that might be applicable to you? Journal your thoughts.

➤ <u>THREE</u>   <u>READ AND CONSIDER THIS QUESTION</u>

~ WHAT DO I SENSE THE LORD WANTS ME TO NOTICE ABOUT HIM?

What can you learn from Jesus' words? His actions? What character qualities do you see in Him? What emotions? What can you learn about His heart? What do you think He might be trying to accomplish? How does He answer questions? What patterns do you see as He lives out His life as a man? What is He trying to communicate to the people around Him? What do you observe in His lived out life? Remember Jesus said in John 12:45 (AMP), *"And whoever sees Me sees the One who sent Me."* To see Jesus is to see God. Journal your thoughts.

WAYS TO READ AND REFLECT

➤ <u>FOUR</u>   <u>READ AND CONSIDER THIS QUESTION</u>

~ WHAT MIGHT THE LORD BE SAYING TO ME, PERSONALLY, TODAY?

God's Word is always personal. It is applicable for your right here, right now, everyday life. No matter your circumstances, God wants to speak into your life. Think about how what you are reading might intersect with what is currently going on in your life. What are you drawn to as you read? We can trust the Holy Spirit to lead us as we listen for what He might want to say to us. John tells us in John 14:26 (AMP), Jesus said, *"But the Helper (Comforter, Advocate, Intercessor—Counselor, Strengthener, Standby), the Holy Spirit, whom the Father will send in My name [in My place, to represent Me and act on My behalf], He will teach you all things. And He will help you remember everything that I have told you."*

What you sense He is telling you could be something new you are learning or it could be something you need to be reminded of. It could be major or it could be something subtle. Journal your thoughts.

➤ <u>FIVE</u>

~ WRITE A PRAYER OF RESPONSE TO THE LORD.

Share your heart with the Lord around what He is showing you. Talk to Him about how His Word is resonating with you today. Be specific. Be honest. He knows what is going on with you so you don't need to hold back.

You might want to write something down to take with you into your day. This could be a word, a phrase, or a passage of scripture, that can bring to mind what God has shown you, when you need it later in the day.

Look for opportunities to share His Word with someone, today. This may or may not involve using words. Remember James 1:25 (NIV), *"But whoever looks intently into the perfect law that gives freedom, and continues in it—not forgetting what they have heard, but doing it— they will be blessed in what they do."* Living our lives, as followers of Jesus, will be eminently tangible, just as the life He lived among us was.

1. John 1:1-14 (ESV)   In the beginning was the Word, and the Word was with God, and the Word was God. ² He was in the beginning with God. ³ All things were made through him, and without him was not any thing made that was made. ⁴ In him was life, and the life was the light of men. ⁵ The light shines in the darkness, and the darkness has not overcome it.

⁶ There was a man sent from God, whose name was John. ⁷ He came as a witness, to bear witness about the light, that all might believe through him. ⁸ He was not the light, but came to bear witness about the light.

⁹ The true light, which gives light to everyone, was coming into the world. ¹⁰ He was in the world, and the world was made through him, yet the world did not know him. ¹¹ He came to his own, and his own people did not receive him. ¹² But to all who did receive him, who believed in his name, he gave the right to become children of God, ¹³ who were born, not of blood nor of the will of the flesh nor of the will of man, but of God.

¹⁴ And the Word became flesh and dwelt among us, and we have seen his glory, glory as of the only Son from the Father, full of grace and truth.

See Hebrews 1:1-4

What are your initial observations from your first reading?

What can you see in people you might recognize in yourself?

What do you sense the Lord wants you to notice about Him?

What might the Lord be saying to you personally, today?

Write a prayer of response to the Lord.

2. Luke 2:1-16 (NLT) At that time the Roman emperor, Augustus, decreed that a census should be taken throughout the Roman Empire. ² (This was the first census taken when Quirinius was governor of Syria.) ³ All returned to their own ancestral towns to register for this census. ⁴ And because Joseph was a descendant of King David, he had to go to Bethlehem in Judea, David's ancient home. He traveled there from the village of Nazareth in Galilee. ⁵ He took with him Mary, to whom he was engaged, who was now expecting a child.

⁶ And while they were there, the time came for her baby to be born. ⁷ She gave birth to her firstborn son. She wrapped him snugly in strips of cloth and laid him in a manger, because there was no lodging available for them.

⁸ That night there were shepherds staying in the fields nearby, guarding their flocks of sheep.⁹ Suddenly, an angel of the Lord appeared among them, and the radiance of the Lord's glory surrounded them. They were terrified, ¹⁰ but the angel reassured them. "Don't be afraid!" he said. "I bring you good news that will bring great joy to all people. ¹¹ The Savior—yes, the Messiah, the Lord—has been born today in Bethlehem, the city of David! ¹² And you will recognize him by this sign: You will find a baby wrapped snugly in strips of cloth, lying in a manger."

¹³ Suddenly, the angel was joined by a vast host of others—the armies of heaven—praising God and saying, ¹⁴ "Glory to God in highest heaven, and peace on earth to those with whom God is pleased."

¹⁵ When the angels had returned to heaven, the shepherds said to each other, "Let's go to Bethlehem! Let's see this thing that has happened, which the Lord has told us about."

¹⁶ They hurried to the village and found Mary and Joseph. And there was the baby, lying in the manger.

See Micah 5:2-5

What are your initial observations from your first reading?

What can you see in people you might recognize in yourself?

What do you sense the Lord wants you to notice about Him?

What might the Lord be saying to you personally, today?

Write a prayer of response to the Lord.

3. Matthew 3:13-17 (ESV) Then Jesus went from Galilee to the Jordan River to be baptized by John. [14] But John tried to talk him out of it. "I am the one who needs to be baptized by you," he said, "so why are you coming to me?"

[15] But Jesus said, "It should be done, for we must carry out all that God requires." So John agreed to baptize him.

[16] After his baptism, as Jesus came up out of the water, the heavens were opened and he saw the Spirit of God descending like a dove and settling on him. [17] And a voice from heaven said, "This is my dearly loved Son, who brings me great joy."

What are your initial observations from your first reading?

What can you see in people you might recognize in yourself?

What do you sense the Lord wants you to notice about Him?

What might the Lord be saying to you personally, today?

Write a prayer of response to the Lord.

4. Luke 4:1-15 (NIV)   Jesus, full of the Holy Spirit, left the Jordan and was led by the Spirit into the wilderness, [2] where for forty days he was tempted by the devil. He ate nothing during those days, and at the end of them he was hungry.

[3] The devil said to him, "If you are the Son of God, tell this stone to become bread."

[4] Jesus answered, "It is written: 'Man shall not live on bread alone.'"

[5] The devil led him up to a high place and showed him in an instant all the kingdoms of the world. [6] And he said to him, "I will give you all their authority and splendor; it has been given to me, and I can give it to anyone I want to. [7] If you worship me, it will all be yours."

[8] Jesus answered, "It is written: 'Worship the Lord your God and serve him only.'"

[9] The devil led him to Jerusalem and had him stand on the highest point of the temple. "If you are the Son of God," he said, "throw yourself down from here. [10] For it is written:

"'He will command his angels concerning you
    to guard you carefully;
[11] they will lift you up in their hands,
    so that you will not strike your foot against a stone.'"

[12] Jesus answered, "It is said: 'Do not put the Lord your God to the test.'"

[13] When the devil had finished all this tempting, he left him until an opportune time.

[14] Jesus returned to Galilee in the power of the Spirit, and news about him spread through the whole countryside. [15] He was teaching in their synagogues, and everyone praised him.

What are your initial observations from your first reading?

What can you see in people you might recognize in yourself?

What do you sense the Lord wants you to notice about Him?

What might the Lord be saying to you personally, today?

Write a prayer of response to the Lord.

5. John 2:1-11 (MSG)   Three days later there was a wedding in the village of Cana in Galilee. Jesus' mother was there. Jesus and his disciples were guests also. When they started running low on wine at the wedding banquet, Jesus' mother told him, "They're just about out of wine."

⁴ Jesus said, "Is that any of our business, Mother—yours or mine? This isn't my time. Don't push me."

⁵ She went ahead anyway, telling the servants, "Whatever he tells you, do it."

⁶⁻⁷ Six stoneware water pots were there, used by the Jews for ritual washings. Each held twenty to thirty gallons. Jesus ordered the servants, "Fill the pots with water." And they filled them to the brim.

⁸ "Now fill your pitchers and take them to the host," Jesus said, and they did.

⁹⁻¹⁰ When the host tasted the water that had become wine (he didn't know what had just happened but the servants, of course, knew), he called out to the bridegroom, "Everybody I know begins with their finest wines and after the guests have had their fill brings in the cheap stuff. But you've saved the best till now!"

¹¹ This act in Cana of Galilee was the first sign Jesus gave, the first glimpse of his glory. And his disciples believed in him.

What are your initial observations from your first reading?

What can you see in people you might recognize in yourself?

What do you sense the Lord wants you to notice about Him?

What might the Lord be saying to you personally, today?

Write a prayer of response to the Lord.

6.   John 3:1-17 (NLT)   There was a man named Nicodemus, a Jewish religious leader who was a Pharisee. [2] After dark one evening, he came to speak with Jesus. "Rabbi," he said, "we all know that God has sent you to teach us. Your miraculous signs are evidence that God is with you."

[3] Jesus replied, "I tell you the truth, unless you are born again, you cannot see the Kingdom of God."

[4] "What do you mean?" exclaimed Nicodemus. "How can an old man go back into his mother's womb and be born again?"

[5] Jesus replied, "I assure you, no one can enter the Kingdom of God without being born of water and the Spirit. [6] Humans can reproduce only human life, but the Holy Spirit gives birth to spiritual life. [7] So don't be surprised when I say, 'You must be born again.' [8] The wind blows wherever it wants. Just as you can hear the wind but can't tell where it comes from or where it is going, so you can't explain how people are born of the Spirit."

[9] "How are these things possible?" Nicodemus asked.

[10] Jesus replied, "You are a respected Jewish teacher, and yet you don't understand these things? [11] I assure you, we tell you what we know and have seen, and yet you won't believe our testimony. [12] But if you don't believe me when I tell you about earthly things, how can you possibly believe if I tell you about heavenly things? [13] No one has ever gone to heaven and returned. But the Son of Man has come down from heaven. [14] And as Moses lifted up the bronze snake on a pole in the wilderness, so the Son of Man must be lifted up, [15] so that everyone who believes in him will have eternal life. [16] "For this is how God loved the world: He gave his one and only Son, so that everyone who believes in him will not perish but have eternal life. [17] God sent his Son into the world not to judge the world, but to save the world through him.

What are your initial observations from your first reading?

What can you see in people you might recognize in yourself?

What do you sense the Lord wants you to notice about Him?

What might the Lord be saying to you personally, today?

Write a prayer of response to the Lord.

7. Luke 4:16-21 (AMP)   So He came to Nazareth, where He had been brought up; and as was His custom, He entered the synagogue on the Sabbath, and stood up to read. [17] The scroll of the prophet Isaiah was handed to Him. He unrolled the scroll and found the place where it was written,

[18] "The Spirit of the Lord is upon Me (the Messiah),

Because He has anointed Me to preach the good news to the poor.

He has sent Me to announce release (pardon, forgiveness) to the captives,

And recovery of sight to the blind,

To set free those who are oppressed (downtrodden, bruised, crushed by tragedy),

[19] to proclaim the favorable year of the Lord

[the day when salvation and the favor of God abound greatly]."

[20] Then He rolled up the scroll [having stopped in the middle of the verse], gave it back to the attendant and sat down [to teach]; and the eyes of all those in the synagogue were [attentively] fixed on Him. [21] He began speaking to them: "Today this Scripture has been fulfilled in your hearing *and* in your presence."

See Isaiah 61:1-7

What are your initial observations from your first reading?

What can you see in people you might recognize in yourself?

What do you sense the Lord wants you to notice about Him?

What might the Lord be saying to you personally, today?

Write a prayer of response to the Lord.

8. Luke 5:1-11 (NLT)   One day as Jesus was preaching on the shore of the Sea of Galilee, great crowds pressed in on him to listen to the word of God. ² He noticed two empty boats at the water's edge, for the fishermen had left them and were washing their nets. ³ Stepping into one of the boats, Jesus asked Simon, its owner, to push it out into the water. So he sat in the boat and taught the crowds from there.

⁴ When he had finished speaking, he said to Simon, "Now go out where it is deeper, and let down your nets to catch some fish."

⁵ "Master," Simon replied, "we worked hard all last night and didn't catch a thing. But if you say so, I'll let the nets down again." ⁶ And this time their nets were so full of fish they began to tear! ⁷ A shout for help brought their partners in the other boat, and soon both boats were filled with fish and on the verge of sinking.

⁸ When Simon Peter realized what had happened, he fell to his knees before Jesus and said, "Oh, Lord, please leave me—I'm such a sinful man." ⁹ For he was awestruck by the number of fish they had caught, as were the others with him. ¹⁰ His partners, James and John, the sons of Zebedee, were also amazed.

Jesus replied to Simon, "Don't be afraid! From now on you'll be fishing for people!" ¹¹ And as soon as they landed, they left everything and followed Jesus.

See Psalm 25:4-5 & Ephesians 5:1-2

What are your initial observations from your first reading?

What can you see in people you might recognize in yourself?

What do you sense the Lord wants you to notice about Him?

What might the Lord be saying to you personally, today?

Write a prayer of response to the Lord.

9. Matthew 6:5-18 (NLT) "When you pray, don't be like the hypocrites who love to pray publicly on street corners and in the synagogues where everyone can see them. I tell you the truth, that is all the reward they will ever get. [6] But when you pray, go away by yourself, shut the door behind you, and pray to your Father in private. Then your Father, who sees everything, will reward you.

[7] "When you pray, don't babble on and on as the Gentiles do. They think their prayers are answered merely by repeating their words again and again. [8] Don't be like them, for your Father knows exactly what you need even before you ask him! [9] Pray like this:

Our Father in heaven,

may your name be kept holy.

[10] May your Kingdom come soon.

May your will be done on earth, as it is in heaven.

[11] Give us today the food we need,

[12] and forgive us our sins,

as we have forgiven those who sin against us.

[13] And don't let us yield to temptation,

but rescue us from the evil one.

[14] "If you forgive those who sin against you, your heavenly Father will forgive you. [15] But if you refuse to forgive others, your Father will not forgive your sins. [16] "And when you fast, don't make it obvious, as the hypocrites do, for they try to look miserable and disheveled so people will admire them for their fasting. I tell you the truth, that is the only reward they will ever get. [17] But when you fast, comb your hair and wash your face. [18] Then no one will notice that you are fasting, except your Father, who knows what you do in private. And your Father, who sees everything, will reward you.

What are your initial observations from your first reading?

What can you see in people you might recognize in yourself?

What do you sense the Lord wants you to notice about Him?

What might the Lord be saying to you personally, today?

Write a prayer of response to the Lord.

10. Matthew 7:24-29 (ESV)   "Everyone then who hears these words of mine and does them will be like a wise man who built his house on the rock. ²⁵ And the rain fell, and the floods came, and the winds blew and beat on that house, but it did not fall, because it had been founded on the rock. ²⁶ And everyone who hears these words of mine and does not do them will be like a foolish man who built his house on the sand. ²⁷ And the rain fell, and the floods came, and the winds blew and beat against that house, and it fell, and great was the fall of it."

²⁸ And when Jesus finished these sayings, the crowds were astonished at his teaching, ²⁹ for he was teaching them as one who had authority, and not as their scribes.

What are your initial observations from your first reading?

What can you see in people you might recognize in yourself?

What do you sense the Lord wants you to notice about Him?

What might the Lord be saying to you personally, today?

Write a prayer of response to the Lord.

11. Luke 7:1-10 (NIV) When Jesus had finished saying all this to the people who were listening, he entered Capernaum. ² There a centurion's servant, whom his master valued highly, was sick and about to die. ³ The centurion heard of Jesus and sent some elders of the Jews to him, asking him to come and heal his servant. ⁴ When they came to Jesus, they pleaded earnestly with him, "This man deserves to have you do this, ⁵ because he loves our nation and has built our synagogue." ⁶ So Jesus went with them.

He was not far from the house when the centurion sent friends to say to him: "Lord, don't trouble yourself, for I do not deserve to have you come under my roof. ⁷ That is why I did not even consider myself worthy to come to you. But say the word, and my servant will be healed. ⁸ For I myself am a man under authority, with soldiers under me. I tell this one, 'Go,' and he goes; and that one, 'Come,' and he comes. I say to my servant, 'Do this,' and he does it."

⁹ When Jesus heard this, he was amazed at him, and turning to the crowd following him, he said, "I tell you, I have not found such great faith even in Israel." ¹⁰ Then the men who had been sent returned to the house and found the servant well.

What are your initial observations from your first reading?

What can you see in people you might recognize in yourself?

What do you sense the Lord wants you to notice about Him?

What might the Lord be saying to you personally, today?

Write a prayer of response to the Lord.

12.   Matthew 11:25-30 (MSG)   Abruptly Jesus broke into prayer: "Thank you, Father, Lord of heaven and earth. You've concealed your ways from sophisticates and know-it-alls, but spelled them out clearly to ordinary people. Yes, Father, that's the way you like to work."

[27] Jesus resumed talking to the people, but now tenderly. "The Father has given me all these things to do and say. This is a unique Father-Son operation, coming out of Father and Son intimacies and knowledge. No one knows the Son the way the Father does, nor the Father the way the Son does. But I'm not keeping it to myself; I'm ready to go over it line by line with anyone willing to listen.

[28-30] "Are you tired? Worn out? Burned out on religion? Come to me. Get away with me and you'll recover your life. I'll show you how to take a real rest. Walk with me and work with me—watch how I do it. Learn the unforced rhythms of grace. I won't lay anything heavy or ill-fitting on you. Keep company with me and you'll learn to live freely and lightly."

See Isaiah 55:1-3

What are your initial observations from your first reading?

What can you see in people you might recognize in yourself?

What do you sense the Lord wants you to notice about Him?

What might the Lord be saying to you personally, today?

Write a prayer of response to the Lord.

13.   Mark 4:10-20 (NIV)   When he was alone, the Twelve and the others around him asked him about the parables.[11] He told them, "The secret of the kingdom of God has been given to you. But to those on the outside everything is said in parables [12] so that,

'"they may be ever seeing but never perceiving,

and ever hearing but never understanding;

otherwise they might turn and be forgiven!'"

[13] Then Jesus said to them, "Don't you understand this parable? How then will you understand any parable? [14] The farmer sows the word. [15] Some people are like seed along the path, where the word is sown. As soon as they hear it, Satan comes and takes away the word that was sown in them. [16] Others, like seed sown on rocky places, hear the word and at once receive it with joy. [17] But since they have no root, they last only a short time. When trouble or persecution comes because of the word, they quickly fall away. [18] Still others, like seed sown among thorns, hear the word; [19] but the worries of this life, the deceitfulness of wealth and the desires for other things come in and choke the word, making it unfruitful. [20] Others, like seed sown on good soil, hear the word, accept it, and produce a crop—some thirty, some sixty, some a hundred times what was sown."

What are your initial observations from your first reading?

What can you see in people you might recognize in yourself?

What do you sense the Lord wants you to notice about Him?

What might the Lord be saying to you personally, today?

Write a prayer of response to the Lord.

14. Mark 4:35-41 (ESV)   On that day, when evening had come, he said to them, "Let us go across to the other side." ³⁶ And leaving the crowd, they took him with them in the boat, just as he was. And other boats were with him. ³⁷ And a great windstorm arose, and the waves were breaking into the boat, so that the boat was already filling. ³⁸ But he was in the stern, asleep on the cushion. And they woke him and said to him, "Teacher, do you not care that we are perishing?" ³⁹ And he awoke and rebuked the wind and said to the sea, "Peace! Be still!" And the wind ceased, and there was a great calm. ⁴⁰ He said to them, "Why are you so afraid? Have you still no faith?" ⁴¹ And they were filled with great fear and said to one another, "Who then is this, that even the wind and the sea obey him?

See Psalm 29:3-4 & Psalm 42:7-8

What are your initial observations from your first reading?

What can you see in people you might recognize in yourself?

What do you sense the Lord wants you to notice about Him?

What might the Lord be saying to you personally, today?

Write a prayer of response to the Lord.

15. Luke 8:43-48 (NLT)   A woman in the crowd had suffered for twelve years with constant bleeding, and she could find no cure. ⁴⁴ Coming up behind Jesus, she touched the fringe of his robe. Immediately, the bleeding stopped.

⁴⁵ "Who touched me?" Jesus asked.

Everyone denied it, and Peter said, "Master, this whole crowd is pressing up against you."

⁴⁶ But Jesus said, "Someone deliberately touched me, for I felt healing power go out from me."

⁴⁷ When the woman realized that she could not stay hidden, she began to tremble and fell to her knees in front of him. The whole crowd heard her explain why she had touched him and that she had been immediately healed. ⁴⁸ "Daughter," he said to her, "your faith has made you well. Go in peace."

What are your initial observations from your first reading?

What can you see in people you might recognize in yourself?

What do you sense the Lord wants you to notice about Him?

What might the Lord be saying to you personally, today?

Write a prayer of response to the Lord.

16.   Mark 6:30-44 (NLT)   The apostles returned to Jesus from their ministry tour and told him all they had done and taught. ³¹ Then Jesus said, "Let's go off by ourselves to a quiet place and rest awhile." He said this because there were so many people coming and going that Jesus and his apostles didn't even have time to eat.

³² So they left by boat for a quiet place, where they could be alone. ³³ But many people recognized them and saw them leaving, and people from many towns ran ahead along the shore and got there ahead of them. ³⁴ Jesus saw the huge crowd as he stepped from the boat, and he had compassion on them because they were like sheep without a shepherd. So he began teaching them many things.

³⁵ Late in the afternoon his disciples came to him and said, "This is a remote place, and it's already getting late. ³⁶ Send the crowds away so they can go to the nearby farms and villages and buy something to eat."

³⁷ But Jesus said, "You feed them."

"With what?" they asked. "We'd have to work for months to earn enough money[a] to buy food for all these people!"

³⁸ "How much bread do you have?" he asked. "Go and find out."

They came back and reported, "We have five loaves of bread and two fish."

³⁹ Then Jesus told the disciples to have the people sit down in groups on the green grass. ⁴⁰ So they sat down in groups of fifty or a hundred.

⁴¹ Jesus took the five loaves and two fish, looked up toward heaven, and blessed them. Then, breaking the loaves into pieces, he kept giving the bread to the disciples so they could distribute it to the people. He also divided the fish for everyone to share. ⁴² They all ate as much as they wanted, ⁴³ and afterward, the disciples picked up twelve baskets of leftover bread and fish. ⁴⁴ A total of 5,000 men and their families were fed.

What are your initial observations from your first reading?

What can you see in people you might recognize in yourself?

What do you sense the Lord wants you to notice about Him?

What might the Lord be saying to you personally, today?

Write a prayer of response to the Lord.

17.   Matthew 14:22-33 (NLT)   Immediately after this, Jesus insisted that his disciples get back into the boat and cross to the other side of the lake, while he sent the people home. ²³ After sending them home, he went up into the hills by himself to pray. Night fell while he was there alone.

²⁴ Meanwhile, the disciples were in trouble far away from land, for a strong wind had risen, and they were fighting heavy waves. ²⁵ About three o'clock in the morning Jesus came toward them, walking on the water. ²⁶ When the disciples saw him walking on the water, they were terrified. In their fear, they cried out, "It's a ghost!"

²⁷ But Jesus spoke to them at once. "Don't be afraid," he said. "Take courage. I am here!"

²⁸ Then Peter called to him, "Lord, if it's really you, tell me to come to you, walking on the water."

²⁹ "Yes, come," Jesus said.

So Peter went over the side of the boat and walked on the water toward Jesus. ³⁰ But when he saw the strong wind and the waves, he was terrified and began to sink. "Save me, Lord!" he shouted.

³¹ Jesus immediately reached out and grabbed him. "You have so little faith," Jesus said. "Why did you doubt me?"

³² When they climbed back into the boat, the wind stopped. ³³ Then the disciples worshiped him. "You really are the Son of God!" they exclaimed.

What are your initial observations from your first reading?

What can you see in people you might recognize in yourself?

What do you sense the Lord wants you to notice about Him?

What might the Lord be saying to you personally, today?

Write a prayer of response to the Lord.

18. John 6:23-35 (NIV) Then some boats from Tiberias landed near the place where the people had eaten the bread after the Lord had given thanks. 24 Once the crowd realized that neither Jesus nor his disciples were there, they got into the boats and went to Capernaum in search of Jesus.

25 When they found him on the other side of the lake, they asked him, "Rabbi, when did you get here?"

26 Jesus answered, "Very truly I tell you, you are looking for me, not because you saw the signs I performed but because you ate the loaves and had your fill. 27 Do not work for food that spoils, but for food that endures to eternal life, which the Son of Man will give you. For on him God the Father has placed his seal of approval."

28 Then they asked him, "What must we do to do the works God requires?"

29 Jesus answered, "The work of God is this: to believe in the one he has sent."

30 So they asked him, "What sign then will you give that we may see it and believe you? What will you do? 31 Our ancestors ate the manna in the wilderness; as it is written: 'He gave them bread from heaven to eat.'[a]"

32 Jesus said to them, "Very truly I tell you, it is not Moses who has given you the bread from heaven, but it is my Father who gives you the true bread from heaven. 33 For the bread of God is the bread that comes down from heaven and gives life to the world."

34 "Sir," they said, "always give us this bread."

35 Then Jesus declared, "I am the bread of life. Whoever comes to me will never go hungry, and whoever believes in me will never be thirsty.

See Matthew 26:26-30

What are your initial observations from your first reading?

What can you see in people you might recognize in yourself?

What do you sense the Lord wants you to notice about Him?

What might the Lord be saying to you personally, today?

Write a prayer of response to the Lord.

19. Matthew 16:13-21 (ESV)   Now when Jesus came into the district of Caesarea Philippi, he asked his disciples, "Who do people say that the Son of Man is?" [14] And they said, "Some say John the Baptist, others say Elijah, and others Jeremiah or one of the prophets." [15] He said to them, "But who do you say that I am?" [16] Simon Peter replied, "You are the Christ, the Son of the living God." [17] And Jesus answered him, "Blessed are you, Simon Bar-Jonah! For flesh and blood has not revealed this to you, but my Father who is in heaven. [18] And I tell you, you are Peter, and on this rock I will build my church, and the gates of hell shall not prevail against it. [19] I will give you the keys of the kingdom of heaven, and whatever you bind on earth shall be bound in heaven, and whatever you loose on earth shall be loosed in heaven." [20] Then he strictly charged the disciples to tell no one that he was the Christ.

[21] From that time Jesus began to show his disciples that he must go to Jerusalem and suffer many things from the elders and chief priests and scribes, and be killed, and on the third day be raised.

What are your initial observations from your first reading?

What can you see in people you might recognize in yourself?

What do you sense the Lord wants you to notice about Him?

What might the Lord be saying to you personally, today?

Write a prayer of response to the Lord.

20.   Matthew 17:1-9 (AMP)   Six days later Jesus took with Him Peter and James and John the brother of James, and led them up on a high mountain by themselves. ² And His appearance changed dramatically in their presence; and His face shone [with heavenly glory, clear and bright] like the sun, and His clothing became as white as light. ³ And behold, Moses and Elijah appeared to them, talking with Jesus. ⁴ Then Peter began to speak and said to Jesus, "Lord, it is good *and* delightful *and* auspicious that we are here; if You wish, I will put up three [sacred] tents here—one for You, one for Moses, and one for Elijah." ⁵ While he was still speaking, behold, a bright cloud overshadowed them, and a voice from the cloud said, "This is My beloved Son, with whom I am well-pleased *and* delighted! Listen to Him!" ⁶ When the disciples heard it, they fell on their faces and were terrified. ⁷ But Jesus came and touched them and said, "Get up, and do not be afraid." ⁸ And when they looked up, they saw no one except Jesus Himself alone.

⁹ And as they were going down the mountain, Jesus commanded them, "Do not tell anyone what you have seen until the Son of Man has been raised from the dead."

See 2 Peter 1:16-18

What are your initial observations from your first reading?

What can you see in people you might recognize in yourself?

What do you sense the Lord wants you to notice about Him?

What might the Lord be saying to you personally, today?

Write a prayer of response to the Lord.

21. John 8:1-11 (AMP)   But Jesus went to the Mount of Olives. ² Early in the morning He came back into the temple [court], and all the people were coming to Him. He sat down and *began* teaching them. ³ Now the scribes and Pharisees brought a woman who had been caught in adultery. They made her stand in the center *of the court,* ⁴ and they said to Him, "Teacher, this woman has been caught in the very act of adultery. ⁵ Now in the Law Moses commanded us to stone such women [to death]. So what do You say [to do with her—what is Your sentence]?" ⁶ They said this to test Him, hoping that they would have grounds for accusing Him. But Jesus stooped down and began writing on the ground with His finger. ⁷ However, when they persisted in questioning Him, He straightened up and said, "He who is without [any] sin among you, let him be the first to throw a stone at her." ⁸ Then He stooped down again and started writing on the ground. ⁹ They listened [to His reply], and they *began* to go out one by one, starting with the oldest ones, until He was left alone, with the woman [standing there before Him] in the center *of the court.* ¹⁰ Straightening up, Jesus said to her, "Woman, where are they? Did no one condemn you?" ¹¹ She answered, "No one, Lord!" And Jesus said, "I do not condemn you either. Go. From now on sin no more."]

See Psalm 103:2-4 & 11-12

What are your initial observations from your first reading?

What can you see in people you might recognize in yourself?

What do you sense the Lord wants you to notice about Him?

What might the Lord be saying to you personally, today?

Write a prayer of response to the Lord.

22. John 8:12-20 (NIV)   When Jesus spoke again to the people, he said, "I am the light of the world. Whoever follows me will never walk in darkness, but will have the light of life."

[13] The Pharisees challenged him, "Here you are, appearing as your own witness; your testimony is not valid."

[14] Jesus answered, "Even if I testify on my own behalf, my testimony is valid, for I know where I came from and where I am going. But you have no idea where I come from or where I am going. [15] You judge by human standards; I pass judgment on no one. [16] But if I do judge, my decisions are true, because I am not alone. I stand with the Father, who sent me. [17] In your own Law it is written that the testimony of two witnesses is true. [18] I am one who testifies for myself; my other witness is the Father, who sent me."

[19] Then they asked him, "Where is your father?"

"You do not know me or my Father," Jesus replied. "If you knew me, you would know my Father also." [20] He spoke these words while teaching in the temple courts near the place where the offerings were put. Yet no one seized him, because his hour had not yet come.

See Isaiah 9:1-3 & Revelation 21:22-27

What are your initial observations from your first reading?

What can you see in people you might recognize in yourself?

What do you sense the Lord wants you to notice about Him?

What might the Lord be saying to you personally, today?

Write a prayer of response to the Lord.

23. Luke 10:38-42 (ESV)   Now as they went on their way, Jesus entered a village. And a woman named Martha welcomed him into her house. 39 And she had a sister called Mary, who sat at the Lord's feet and listened to his teaching. 40 But Martha was distracted with much serving. And she went up to him and said, "Lord, do you not care that my sister has left me to serve alone? Tell her then to help me." 41 But the Lord answered her, "Martha, Martha, you are anxious and troubled about many things, 42 but one thing is necessary. Mary has chosen the good portion, which will not be taken away from her."

See Hebrews 12:2-3

What are your initial observations from your first reading?

What can you see in people you might recognize in yourself?

What do you sense the Lord wants you to notice about Him?

What might the Lord be saying to you personally, today?

Write a prayer of response to the Lord.

24. John 10:1-16 (MSG) "Let me set this before you as plainly as I can. If a person climbs over or through the fence of a sheep pen instead of going through the gate, you know he's up to no good—a sheep rustler! The shepherd walks right up to the gate. The gatekeeper opens the gate to him and the sheep recognize his voice. He calls his own sheep by name and leads them out. When he gets them all out, he leads them and they follow because they are familiar with his voice. They won't follow a stranger's voice but will scatter because they aren't used to the sound of it."

6-10 Jesus told this simple story, but they had no idea what he was talking about. So he tried again. "I'll be explicit, then. I am the Gate for the sheep. All those others are up to no good—sheep stealers, every one of them. But the sheep didn't listen to them. I am the Gate. Anyone who goes through me will be cared for—will freely go in and out, and find pasture. A thief is only there to steal and kill and destroy. I came so they can have real and eternal life, more and better life than they ever dreamed of.

11-13 "I am the Good Shepherd. The Good Shepherd puts the sheep before himself, sacrifices himself if necessary. A hired man is not a real shepherd. The sheep mean nothing to him. He sees a wolf come and runs for it, leaving the sheep to be ravaged and scattered by the wolf. He's only in it for the money. The sheep don't matter to him. "I am the Good Shepherd. I know my own sheep and my own sheep know me. In the same way, the Father knows me and I know the Father. I put the sheep before myself, sacrificing myself if necessary. You need to know that I have other sheep in addition to those in this pen. I need to gather and bring them, too. They'll also recognize my voice. Then it will be one flock, one Shepherd.

See Psalm 23

What are your initial observations from your first reading?

What can you see in people you might recognize in yourself?

What do you sense the Lord wants you to notice about Him?

What might the Lord be saying to you personally, today?

Write a prayer of response to the Lord.

25. Luke 15:1-7 (MSG)   By this time a lot of men and women of doubtful reputation were hanging around Jesus, listening intently. The Pharisees and religion scholars were not pleased, not at all pleased. They growled, "He takes in sinners and eats meals with them, treating them like old friends." Their grumbling triggered this story.

4-7 "Suppose one of you had a hundred sheep and lost one. Wouldn't you leave the ninety-nine in the wilderness and go after the lost one until you found it? When found, you can be sure you would put it across your shoulders, rejoicing, and when you got home call in your friends and neighbors, saying, 'Celebrate with me! I've found my lost sheep!' Count on it—there's more joy in heaven over one sinner's rescued life than over ninety-nine good people in no need of rescue.

What are your initial observations from your first reading?

What can you see in people you might recognize in yourself?

What do you sense the Lord wants you to notice about Him?

What might the Lord be saying to you personally, today?

Write a prayer of response to the Lord.

26. Luke 15:11-24 (NIV) Jesus continued: "There was a man who had two sons. ¹²The younger one said to his father, 'Father, give me my share of the estate.' So he divided his property between them.

¹³ "Not long after that, the younger son got together all he had, set off for a distant country and there squandered his wealth in wild living. ¹⁴After he had spent everything, there was a severe famine in that whole country, and he began to be in need. ¹⁵So he went and hired himself out to a citizen of that country, who sent him to his fields to feed pigs. ¹⁶He longed to fill his stomach with the pods that the pigs were eating, but no one gave him anything.

¹⁷ "When he came to his senses, he said, 'How many of my father's hired servants have food to spare, and here I am starving to death! ¹⁸I will set out and go back to my father and say to him: Father, I have sinned against heaven and against you. ¹⁹I am no longer worthy to be called your son; make me like one of your hired servants.' ²⁰So he got up and went to his father.

"But while he was still a long way off, his father saw him and was filled with compassion for him; he ran to his son, threw his arms around him and kissed him.

²¹ "The son said to him, 'Father, I have sinned against heaven and against you. I am no longer worthy to be called your son.'

²² "But the father said to his servants, 'Quick! Bring the best robe and put it on him. Put a ring on his finger and sandals on his feet. ²³Bring the fattened calf and kill it. Let's have a feast and celebrate. ²⁴For this son of mine was dead and is alive again; he was lost and is found.' So they began to celebrate.

What are your initial observations from your first reading?

What can you see in people you might recognize in yourself?

What do you sense the Lord wants you to notice about Him?

What might the Lord be saying to you personally, today?

Write a prayer of response to the Lord.

27. John 11:1-20 (NLT)   A man named Lazarus was sick. He lived in Bethany with his sisters, Mary and Martha. 2 This is the Mary who later poured the expensive perfume on the Lord's feet and wiped them with her hair. Her brother, Lazarus, was sick. 3 So the two sisters sent a message to Jesus telling him, "Lord, your dear friend is very sick."

4 But when Jesus heard about it he said, "Lazarus's sickness will not end in death. No, it happened for the glory of God so that the Son of God will receive glory from this." 5 So although Jesus loved Martha, Mary, and Lazarus, 6 he stayed where he was for the next two days. 7 Finally, he said to his disciples, "Let's go back to Judea."

8 But his disciples objected. "Rabbi," they said, "only a few days ago the people in Judea were trying to stone you. Are you going there again?"

9 Jesus replied, "There are twelve hours of daylight every day. During the day people can walk safely. They can see because they have the light of this world. 10 But at night there is danger of stumbling because they have no light." 11 Then he said, "Our friend Lazarus has fallen asleep, but now I will go and wake him up."

12 The disciples said, "Lord, if he is sleeping, he will soon get better!" 13 They thought Jesus meant Lazarus was simply sleeping, but Jesus meant Lazarus had died.

14 So he told them plainly, "Lazarus is dead. 15 And for your sakes, I'm glad I wasn't there, for now you will really believe. Come, let's go see him."

16 Thomas, nicknamed the Twin, said to his fellow disciples, "Let's go, too—and die with Jesus."

17 When Jesus arrived at Bethany, he was told that Lazarus had already been in his grave for four days. 18 Bethany was only a few miles down the road from Jerusalem, 19 and many of the people had come to console Martha and Mary in their loss. 20 When Martha got word that Jesus was coming, she went to meet him. But Mary stayed in the house.

What are your initial observations from your first reading?

What can you see in people you might recognize in yourself?

What do you sense the Lord wants you to notice about Him?

What might the Lord be saying to you personally, today?

Write a prayer of response to the Lord.

28.   John 11:21-37 (NLT)   Martha said to Jesus, "Lord, if only you had been here, my brother would not have died. 22 But even now I know that God will give you whatever you ask."

23 Jesus told her, "Your brother will rise again."

24 "Yes," Martha said, "he will rise when everyone else rises, at the last day."

25 Jesus told her, "I am the resurrection and the life. Anyone who believes in me will live, even after dying. 26 Everyone who lives in me and believes in me will never ever die. Do you believe this, Martha?"

27 "Yes, Lord," she told him. "I have always believed you are the Messiah, the Son of God, the one who has come into the world from God." 28 Then she returned to Mary. She called Mary aside from the mourners and told her, "The Teacher is here and wants to see you." 29 So Mary immediately went to him.

30 Jesus had stayed outside the village, at the place where Martha met him. 31 When the people who were at the house consoling Mary saw her leave so hastily, they assumed she was going to Lazarus's grave to weep. So they followed her there. 32 When Mary arrived and saw Jesus, she fell at his feet and said, "Lord, if only you had been here, my brother would not have died."

33 When Jesus saw her weeping and saw the other people wailing with her, a deep anger welled up within him, and he was deeply troubled. 34 "Where have you put him?" he asked them.

They told him, "Lord, come and see." 35 Then Jesus wept. 36 The people who were standing nearby said, "See how much he loved him!" 37 But some said, "This man healed a blind man. Couldn't he have kept Lazarus from dying?"

See Psalm 34:18

What are your initial observations from your first reading?

What can you see in people you might recognize in yourself?

What do you sense the Lord wants you to notice about Him?

What might the Lord be saying to you personally, today?

Write a prayer of response to the Lord.

29. John 11:38-44 (NLT)   Jesus was still angry as he arrived at the tomb, a cave with a stone rolled across its entrance. ³⁹ "Roll the stone aside," Jesus told them. But Martha, the dead man's sister, protested, "Lord, he has been dead for four days. The smell will be terrible."

⁴⁰ Jesus responded, "Didn't I tell you that you would see God's glory if you believe?"

⁴¹ So they rolled the stone aside. Then Jesus looked up to heaven and said, "Father, thank you for hearing me. ⁴² You always hear me, but I said it out loud for the sake of all these people standing here, so that they will believe you sent me."

⁴³ Then Jesus shouted, "Lazarus, come out!"

⁴⁴ And the dead man came out, his hands and feet bound in graveclothes, his face wrapped in a headcloth. Jesus told them, "Unwrap him and let him go!"

What are your initial observations from your first reading?

What can you see in people you might recognize in yourself?

What do you sense the Lord wants you to notice about Him?

What might the Lord be saying to you personally, today?

Write a prayer of response to the Lord.

30. Luke 18:35-43 (ESV)   As he drew near to Jericho, a blind man was sitting by the roadside begging. 36 And hearing a crowd going by, he inquired what this meant. 37 They told him, "Jesus of Nazareth is passing by." 38 And he cried out, "Jesus, Son of David, have mercy on me!" 39 And those who were in front rebuked him, telling him to be silent. But he cried out all the more, "Son of David, have mercy on me!" 40 And Jesus stopped and commanded him to be brought to him. And when he came near, he asked him, 41 "What do you want me to do for you?" He said, "Lord, let me recover my sight." 42 And Jesus said to him, "Recover your sight; your faith has made you well." 43 And immediately he recovered his sight and followed him, glorifying God. And all the people, when they saw it, gave praise to God.

What are your initial observations from your first reading?

What can you see in people you might recognize in yourself?

What do you sense the Lord wants you to notice about Him?

What might the Lord be saying to you personally, today?

Write a prayer of response to the Lord.

31. Luke 19:28-40 (NIV)   After Jesus had said this, he went on ahead, going up to Jerusalem. 29 As he approached Bethphage and Bethany at the hill called the Mount of Olives, he sent two of his disciples, saying to them, 30 "Go to the village ahead of you, and as you enter it, you will find a colt tied there, which no one has ever ridden. Untie it and bring it here. 31 If anyone asks you, 'Why are you untying it?' say, 'The Lord needs it.'"

32 Those who were sent ahead went and found it just as he had told them. 33 As they were untying the colt, its owners asked them, "Why are you untying the colt?"

34 They replied, "The Lord needs it."

35 They brought it to Jesus, threw their cloaks on the colt and put Jesus on it. 36 As he went along, people spread their cloaks on the road.

37 When he came near the place where the road goes down the Mount of Olives, the whole crowd of disciples began joyfully to praise God in loud voices for all the miracles they had seen:

38 "Blessed is the king who comes in the name of the Lord!"[a]

"Peace in heaven and glory in the highest!"

39 Some of the Pharisees in the crowd said to Jesus, "Teacher, rebuke your disciples!"

40 "I tell you," he replied, "if they keep quiet, the stones will cry out."

See Zechariah 9:9

What are your initial observations from your first reading?

What can you see in people you might recognize in yourself?

What do you sense the Lord wants you to notice about Him?

What might the Lord be saying to you personally, today?

Write a prayer of response to the Lord.

32. John 12:20-33 (ESV)   Now among those who went up to worship at the feast were some Greeks. ²¹ So these came to Philip, who was from Bethsaida in Galilee, and asked him, "Sir, we wish to see Jesus." ²² Philip went and told Andrew; Andrew and Philip went and told Jesus. ²³ And Jesus answered them, "The hour has come for the Son of Man to be glorified. ²⁴ Truly, truly, I say to you, unless a grain of wheat falls into the earth and dies, it remains alone; but if it dies, it bears much fruit. ²⁵ Whoever loves his life loses it, and whoever hates his life in this world will keep it for eternal life. ²⁶ If anyone serves me, he must follow me; and where I am, there will my servant be also. If anyone serves me, the Father will honor him.

²⁷ "Now is my soul troubled. And what shall I say? 'Father, save me from this hour'? But for this purpose I have come to this hour. ²⁸ Father, glorify your name." Then a voice came from heaven: "I have glorified it, and I will glorify it again." ²⁹ The crowd that stood there and heard it said that it had thundered. Others said, "An angel has spoken to him." ³⁰ Jesus answered, "This voice has come for your sake, not mine. ³¹ Now is the judgment of this world; now will the ruler of this world be cast out. ³² And I, when I am lifted up from the earth, will draw all people to myself." ³³ He said this to show by what kind of death he was going to die.

What are your initial observations from your first reading?

What can you see in people you might recognize in yourself?

What do you sense the Lord wants you to notice about Him?

What might the Lord be saying to you personally, today?

Write a prayer of response to the Lord.

33. Mark 12:28-34 (NIV) One of the teachers of the law came and heard them debating. Noticing that Jesus had given them a good answer, he asked him, "Of all the commandments, which is the most important?"

29 "The most important one," answered Jesus, "is this:

'Hear, O Israel: The Lord our God, the Lord is one.

30 Love the Lord your God with all your heart

and with all your soul and with all your mind

and with all your strength.'

31 The second is this:

'Love your neighbor as yourself.'

There is no commandment greater than these."

32 "Well said, teacher," the man replied. "You are right in saying that God is one and there is no other but him. 33 To love him with all your heart, with all your understanding and with all your strength, and to love your neighbor as yourself is more important than all burnt offerings and sacrifices."

34 When Jesus saw that he had answered wisely, he said to him, "You are not far from the kingdom of God." And from then on no one dared ask him any more questions.

See Deuteronomy 6:4-5

What are your initial observations from your first reading?

What can you see in people you might recognize in yourself?

What do you sense the Lord wants you to notice about Him?

What might the Lord be saying to you personally, today?

Write a prayer of response to the Lord.

34. John 13:1-17 (NLT)   Before the Passover celebration, Jesus knew that his hour had come to leave this world and return to his Father. He had loved his disciples during his ministry on earth, and now he loved them to the very end. ² It was time for supper, and the devil had already prompted Judas, son of Simon Iscariot, to betray Jesus. ³ Jesus knew that the Father had given him authority over everything and that he had come from God and would return to God. ⁴ So he got up from the table, took off his robe, wrapped a towel around his waist, ⁵ and poured water into a basin. Then he began to wash the disciples' feet, drying them with the towel he had around him.

⁶ When Jesus came to Simon Peter, Peter said to him, "Lord, are you going to wash my feet?" ⁷ Jesus replied, "You don't understand now what I am doing, but someday you will."

⁸ "No," Peter protested, "you will never ever wash my feet!" Jesus replied, "Unless I wash you, you won't belong to me." ⁹ Simon Peter exclaimed, "Then wash my hands and head as well, Lord, not just my feet!"

¹⁰ Jesus replied, "A person who has bathed all over does not need to wash, except for the feet, to be entirely clean. And you disciples are clean, but not all of you." ¹¹ For Jesus knew who would betray him. That is what he meant when he said, "Not all of you are clean."

¹² After washing their feet, he put on his robe again and sat down and asked, "Do you understand what I was doing? ¹³ You call me 'Teacher' and 'Lord,' and you are right, because that's what I am. ¹⁴ And since I, your Lord and Teacher, have washed your feet, you ought to wash each other's feet. ¹⁵ I have given you an example to follow. Do as I have done to you. ¹⁶ I tell you the truth, slaves are not greater than their master. Nor is the messenger more important than the one who sends the message. ¹⁷ Now that you know these things, God will bless you for doing them.

What are your initial observations from your first reading?

What can you see in people you might recognize in yourself?

What do you sense the Lord wants you to notice about Him?

What might the Lord be saying to you personally, today?

Write a prayer of response to the Lord.

35. John 15:1-17 (NIV) "I am the true vine, and my Father is the gardener. ² He cuts off every branch in me that bears no fruit, while every branch that does bear fruit he prunes so that it will be even more fruitful. ³ You are already clean because of the word I have spoken to you. ⁴ Remain in me, as I also remain in you. No branch can bear fruit by itself; it must remain in the vine. Neither can you bear fruit unless you remain in me.

⁵ "I am the vine; you are the branches. If you remain in me and I in you, you will bear much fruit; apart from me you can do nothing. ⁶ If you do not remain in me, you are like a branch that is thrown away and withers; such branches are picked up, thrown into the fire and burned. ⁷ If you remain in me and my words remain in you, ask whatever you wish, and it will be done for you. ⁸ This is to my Father's glory, that you bear much fruit, showing yourselves to be my disciples.

⁹ "As the Father has loved me, so have I loved you. Now remain in my love. ¹⁰ If you keep my commands, you will remain in my love, just as I have kept my Father's commands and remain in his love. ¹¹ I have told you this so that my joy may be in you and that your joy may be complete. ¹² My command is this: Love each other as I have loved you. ¹³ Greater love has no one than this: to lay down one's life for one's friends. ¹⁴ You are my friends if you do what I command. ¹⁵ I no longer call you servants, because a servant does not know his master's business. Instead, I have called you friends, for everything that I learned from my Father I have made known to you. ¹⁶ You did not choose me, but I chose you and appointed you so that you might go and bear fruit—fruit that will last—and so that whatever you ask in my name the Father will give you. ¹⁷ This is my command: Love each other.

See Ephesians 3:16-18

What are your initial observations from your first reading?

What can you see in people you might recognize in yourself?

What do you sense the Lord wants you to notice about Him?

What might the Lord be saying to you personally, today?

Write a prayer of response to the Lord.

36. Mark 14:32-46 (ESV)   And they went to a place called Gethsemane. And he said to his disciples, "Sit here while I pray." 33 And he took with him Peter and James and John, and began to be greatly distressed and troubled. 34 And he said to them, "My soul is very sorrowful, even to death. Remain here and watch." 35 And going a little farther, he fell on the ground and prayed that, if it were possible, the hour might pass from him. 36 And he said, "Abba, Father, all things are possible for you. Remove this cup from me. Yet not what I will, but what you will." 37 And he came and found them sleeping, and he said to Peter, "Simon, are you asleep? Could you not watch one hour? 38 Watch and pray that you may not enter into temptation. The spirit indeed is willing, but the flesh is weak." 39 And again he went away and prayed, saying the same words. 40 And again he came and found them sleeping, for their eyes were very heavy, and they did not know what to answer him. 41 And he came the third time and said to them, "Are you still sleeping and taking your rest? It is enough; the hour has come. The Son of Man is betrayed into the hands of sinners. 42 Rise, let us be going; see, my betrayer is at hand."

43 And immediately, while he was still speaking, Judas came, one of the twelve, and with him a crowd with swords and clubs, from the chief priests and the scribes and the elders. 44 Now the betrayer had given them a sign, saying, "The one I will kiss is the man. Seize him and lead him away under guard." 45 And when he came, he went up to him at once and said, "Rabbi!" And he kissed him. 46 And they laid hands on him and seized him.

What are your initial observations from your first reading?

What can you see in people you might recognize in yourself?

What do you sense the Lord wants you to notice about Him?

What might the Lord be saying to you personally, today?

Write a prayer of response to the Lord.

37. Luke 23:32-43 (NIV) Two other men, both criminals, were also led out with him to be executed. 33 When they came to the place called the Skull, they crucified him there, along with the criminals—one on his right, the other on his left. 34 Jesus said, "Father, forgive them, for they do not know what they are doing." And they divided up his clothes by casting lots.

35 The people stood watching, and the rulers even sneered at him. They said, "He saved others; let him save himself if he is God's Messiah, the Chosen One."

36 The soldiers also came up and mocked him. They offered him wine vinegar 37 and said, "If you are the king of the Jews, save yourself."

38 There was a written notice above him, which read: this is the king of the jews.

39 One of the criminals who hung there hurled insults at him: "Aren't you the Messiah? Save yourself and us!"

40 But the other criminal rebuked him. "Don't you fear God," he said, "since you are under the same sentence? 41 We are punished justly, for we are getting what our deeds deserve. But this man has done nothing wrong."

42 Then he said, "Jesus, remember me when you come into your kingdom."

43 Jesus answered him, "Truly I tell you, today you will be with me in paradise."

What are your initial observations from your first reading?

What can you see in people you might recognize in yourself?

What do you sense the Lord wants you to notice about Him?

What might the Lord be saying to you personally, today?

Write a prayer of response to the Lord.

38. Matthew 28:1-7 (NLT)   Early on Sunday morning, as the new day was dawning, Mary Magdalene and the other Mary went out to visit the tomb.

² Suddenly there was a great earthquake! For an angel of the Lord came down from heaven, rolled aside the stone, and sat on it. ³ His face shone like lightning, and his clothing was as white as snow. ⁴ The guards shook with fear when they saw him, and they fell into a dead faint.

⁵ Then the angel spoke to the women. "Don't be afraid!" he said. "I know you are looking for Jesus, who was crucified. ⁶ He isn't here! He is risen from the dead, just as he said would happen. Come, see where his body was lying. ⁷ And now, go quickly and tell his disciples that he has risen from the dead, and he is going ahead of you to Galilee. You will see him there. Remember what I have told you."

What are your initial observations from your first reading?

What can you see in people you might recognize in yourself?

What do you sense the Lord wants you to notice about Him?

What might the Lord be saying to you personally, today?

Write a prayer of response to the Lord.

39. John 21:1-14 (ESV)   After this Jesus revealed himself again to the disciples by the Sea of Tiberias, and he revealed himself in this way. [2] Simon Peter, Thomas (called the Twin), Nathanael of Cana in Galilee, the sons of Zebedee, and two others of his disciples were together. [3] Simon Peter said to them, "I am going fishing." They said to him, "We will go with you." They went out and got into the boat, but that night they caught nothing.

[4] Just as day was breaking, Jesus stood on the shore; yet the disciples did not know that it was Jesus. [5] Jesus said to them, "Children, do you have any fish?" They answered him, "No." [6] He said to them, "Cast the net on the right side of the boat, and you will find some." So they cast it, and now they were not able to haul it in, because of the quantity of fish. [7] That disciple whom Jesus loved therefore said to Peter, "It is the Lord!" When Simon Peter heard that it was the Lord, he put on his outer garment, for he was stripped for work, and threw himself into the sea. [8] The other disciples came in the boat, dragging the net full of fish, for they were not far from the land, but about a hundred yards off.

[9] When they got out on land, they saw a charcoal fire in place, with fish laid out on it, and bread. [10] Jesus said to them, "Bring some of the fish that you have just caught." [11] So Simon Peter went aboard and hauled the net ashore, full of large fish, 153 of them. And although there were so many, the net was not torn. [12] Jesus said to them, "Come and have breakfast. "Now none of the disciples dared ask him, "Who are you?" They knew it was the Lord. [13] Jesus came and took the bread and gave it to them, and so with the fish. [14] This was now the third time that Jesus was revealed to the disciples after he was raised from the dead.

See Mark 1:16-17

What are your initial observations from your first reading?

What can you see in people you might recognize in yourself?

What do you sense the Lord wants you to notice about Him?

What might the Lord be saying to you personally, today?

Write a prayer of response to the Lord.

40. Matthew 28:16-20 (AMP)   Now the eleven disciples went to Galilee, to the mountain which Jesus had designated. [17] And when they saw Him, they worshiped *Him*; but some doubted [that it was really He]. [18] Jesus came up and said to them, "All authority (all power of absolute rule) in heaven and on earth has been given to Me. [19] Go therefore and make disciples of all the nations [help the people to learn of Me, believe in Me, and obey My words], baptizing them in the name of the Father and of the Son and of the Holy Spirit, [20] teaching them to observe everything that I have commanded you; and lo, I am with you always [remaining with you perpetually— regardless of circumstance, and on every occasion], even to the end of the age."

See Matthew 1:23 & Deuteronomy 31:6

Mark 16:19-20 (AMP)   So then, when the Lord Jesus had spoken to them, He was taken up into heaven and sat down at the right hand of God. [20] And they went out and preached everywhere, while the Lord was working with them and confirming the word by the signs that followed.]

See Romans 8:31-39

What are your initial observations from your first reading?

What can you see in people you might recognize in yourself?

What do you sense the Lord wants you to notice about Him?

What might the Lord be saying to you personally, today?

Write a prayer of response to the Lord.

Things I want to remember from this Bible Study:

Made in the USA
Columbia, SC
02 February 2024

31329712R00054